50 Classic French Dishes for Home

By: Kelly Johnson

Table of Contents

- Coq au Vin
- Boeuf Bourguignon
- Ratatouille
- Cassoulet
- Bouillabaisse
- Duck Confit
- Quiche Lorraine
- Croque Monsieur
- Croque Madame
- Tartiflette
- Salade Niçoise
- Chateaubriand Steak
- French Onion Soup
- Blanquette de Veau
- Sole Meunière
- Pissaladière
- Pot-au-Feu
- Brandade de Morue
- Poulet Basquaise
- Tarte Tatin
- Mille-Feuille
- Crêpes Suzette
- Madeleines
- Clafoutis
- Pâté en Croûte
- Escargots de Bourgogne
- Hachis Parmentier
- Andouillette
- Soufflé au Fromage
- Choucroute Garnie
- Tarte Flambée
- Boudin Noir aux Pommes
- Rillettes de Porc
- Oeufs en Meurette
- Pâté de Campagne

- Frisée aux Lardons
- Gâteau Basque
- Île Flottante
- Pain Perdu
- Crème Brûlée
- Galettes Bretonnes
- Boulette d'Avesnes
- Gratin Dauphinois
- Saucisson Lyonnais
- Daube Provençale
- Navarin d'Agneau
- Gigot d'Agneau
- Vol-au-Vent
- Aligot
- Canard à l'Orange

Coq au Vin (French Chicken in Wine)

Ingredients:

- 4 bone-in, skin-on chicken thighs
- 4 bone-in, skin-on chicken drumsticks
- Salt and freshly ground black pepper (to taste)
- 2 tbsp olive oil
- 4 oz pancetta or bacon, diced
- 1 small onion, chopped
- 2 cloves garlic, minced
- 2 cups red wine (Burgundy or Pinot Noir)
- 1 cup chicken broth
- 2 tbsp tomato paste
- 1 bay leaf
- 4 sprigs fresh thyme (or 1 tsp dried thyme)
- 8 oz cremini or button mushrooms, sliced
- 12 pearl onions, peeled
- 2 tbsp unsalted butter
- 2 tbsp all-purpose flour
- Fresh parsley for garnish

Instructions:

1. **Prepare the Chicken:**
    - Season the chicken pieces with salt and pepper.
    - In a large Dutch oven, heat olive oil over medium-high heat.
    - Brown the chicken on all sides (about 5 minutes per side). Remove and set aside.
2. **Cook the Pancetta & Vegetables:**
    - In the same pot, cook the pancetta until crispy.
    - Add the chopped onion and garlic, cooking until softened (about 2 minutes).
3. **Deglaze & Simmer:**
    - Pour in the wine and chicken broth, scraping up any browned bits from the bottom.
    - Stir in tomato paste, bay leaf, and thyme.
    - Return the chicken to the pot. Bring to a boil, then reduce to a simmer. Cover and cook for 45 minutes.
4. **Prepare Mushrooms & Pearl Onions:**

- In a separate pan, melt butter over medium heat.
- Add mushrooms and pearl onions, cooking until golden brown.
- Sprinkle with flour, stirring to coat, then transfer to the Dutch oven.

5. **Final Simmer & Serve:**
    - Simmer uncovered for another 15 minutes to thicken the sauce.
    - Remove bay leaf and thyme sprigs.
    - Garnish with fresh parsley and serve hot with crusty bread or mashed potatoes.

Coq au Vin (French Chicken in Wine)

Ingredients:

- 4 bone-in, skin-on chicken thighs
- 4 bone-in, skin-on chicken drumsticks
- Salt and freshly ground black pepper (to taste)
- 2 tbsp olive oil
- 4 oz pancetta or bacon, diced
- 1 small onion, chopped
- 2 cloves garlic, minced
- 2 cups red wine (Burgundy or Pinot Noir)
- 1 cup chicken broth
- 2 tbsp tomato paste
- 1 bay leaf
- 4 sprigs fresh thyme (or 1 tsp dried thyme)
- 8 oz cremini or button mushrooms, sliced
- 12 pearl onions, peeled
- 2 tbsp unsalted butter
- 2 tbsp all-purpose flour
- Fresh parsley for garnish

Instructions:

1. **Prepare the Chicken:** Season the chicken with salt and pepper, brown in olive oil, and set aside.
2. **Cook the Pancetta & Vegetables:** Crisp the pancetta, then sauté onions and garlic.
3. **Deglaze & Simmer:** Add wine, broth, tomato paste, and herbs; return chicken and simmer for 45 minutes.
4. **Prepare Mushrooms & Pearl Onions:** Sauté in butter, mix with flour, and add to the Dutch oven.
5. **Final Simmer & Serve:** Cook uncovered for 15 minutes, garnish with parsley, and serve hot.

Boeuf Bourguignon (French Beef Stew in Red Wine)

Ingredients:

- 2 lbs beef chuck, cut into cubes
- Salt and freshly ground black pepper (to taste)
- 2 tbsp olive oil
- 6 oz pancetta or bacon, diced
- 1 large onion, chopped
- 2 carrots, sliced
- 3 cloves garlic, minced
- 2 tbsp tomato paste
- 2 tbsp all-purpose flour
- 2 cups red wine (Burgundy or Pinot Noir)
- 1 cup beef broth
- 1 bay leaf
- 4 sprigs fresh thyme
- 8 oz mushrooms, quartered
- 12 pearl onions, peeled
- 2 tbsp unsalted butter

Instructions:

1. **Brown the Beef:** Season and sear beef cubes, then set aside.
2. **Sauté Aromatics:** Cook pancetta, onions, carrots, and garlic.
3. **Deglaze & Simmer:** Stir in tomato paste and flour, then add wine, broth, and herbs.
4. **Slow Cook:** Return beef, cover, and simmer for 2-3 hours.
5. **Prepare Mushrooms & Pearl Onions:** Sauté in butter, then mix into the stew. Simmer for 20 minutes and serve.

Ratatouille (Provençal Vegetable Stew)

Ingredients:

- 1 eggplant, diced
- 1 zucchini, sliced
- 1 red bell pepper, chopped
- 1 yellow bell pepper, chopped
- 1 onion, chopped
- 3 cloves garlic, minced
- 4 large tomatoes, chopped
- 1/4 cup olive oil
- 1 tsp dried thyme
- 1 tsp dried oregano
- Salt and freshly ground black pepper (to taste)
- Fresh basil for garnish

Instructions:

1. **Sauté the Vegetables:** Cook onions and garlic in olive oil, then add bell peppers and eggplant.
2. **Add Tomatoes & Herbs:** Stir in tomatoes, zucchini, thyme, and oregano.
3. **Simmer:** Cover and cook on low heat for 30-40 minutes, stirring occasionally.
4. **Season & Serve:** Adjust salt and pepper, garnish with fresh basil, and serve warm.

Cassoulet (French Slow-Cooked Bean and Meat Stew)

Ingredients:

- 1 lb dried white beans (soaked overnight)
- 2 tbsp olive oil
- 1 lb pork shoulder, cut into chunks
- 4 duck confit legs (or chicken thighs)
- 1/2 lb smoked sausage, sliced
- 1 onion, chopped
- 3 cloves garlic, minced
- 2 carrots, chopped
- 1 can (14 oz) diced tomatoes
- 4 cups chicken broth
- 1 bay leaf
- 4 sprigs fresh thyme
- Salt and freshly ground black pepper (to taste)
- 1 cup breadcrumbs

Instructions:

1. **Prepare the Beans:** Drain and rinse soaked beans.
2. **Brown the Meat:** Sear pork, duck, and sausage in olive oil, then set aside.
3. **Sauté Aromatics:** Cook onions, carrots, and garlic until soft.
4. **Simmer:** Combine beans, meat, tomatoes, broth, and herbs; simmer for 2 hours.
5. **Bake:** Transfer to an ovenproof dish, top with breadcrumbs, and bake at 375°F (190°C) for 30 minutes.

Bouillabaisse (Provençal Fish Stew)

Ingredients:

- 1 lb firm white fish (cod, halibut, or snapper), cut into chunks
- ½ lb mussels, cleaned
- ½ lb shrimp, peeled and deveined
- 1 onion, chopped
- 2 leeks, sliced
- 3 cloves garlic, minced
- 4 large tomatoes, chopped
- 4 cups fish stock
- 1 cup dry white wine
- 2 tbsp olive oil
- 1 tsp saffron threads
- 1 tsp dried thyme
- 1 bay leaf
- Salt and freshly ground black pepper (to taste)
- Fresh parsley for garnish

Instructions:

1. **Sauté Aromatics:** Heat olive oil in a large pot and cook onions, leeks, and garlic.
2. **Add Tomatoes & Liquids:** Stir in tomatoes, fish stock, wine, saffron, thyme, and bay leaf. Bring to a simmer.
3. **Cook Seafood:** Add fish and simmer for 10 minutes, then add mussels and shrimp, cooking until mussels open.
4. **Season & Serve:** Remove bay leaf, adjust seasoning, garnish with parsley, and serve with crusty bread.

Duck Confit (Slow-Cooked Duck)

Ingredients:

- 4 duck legs
- 2 tbsp kosher salt
- 4 cloves garlic, minced
- 1 tbsp fresh thyme leaves
- 2 cups duck fat (or substitute with olive oil)
- Freshly ground black pepper

Instructions:

1. **Cure the Duck:** Rub duck legs with salt, garlic, and thyme. Cover and refrigerate overnight.
2. **Slow Cook:** Rinse off salt, pat dry, and submerge in duck fat. Bake at 250°F (120°C) for 3 hours.
3. **Crisp & Serve:** Remove from fat, sear skin-side down in a hot pan, and serve with roasted potatoes.

Quiche Lorraine (Savory Egg and Bacon Tart)

Ingredients:

- 1 pre-made pie crust
- 6 oz bacon, cooked and crumbled
- 1 cup heavy cream
- 3 large eggs
- ½ cup Gruyère cheese, shredded
- Salt and pepper to taste
- Pinch of nutmeg

Instructions:

1. **Pre-Bake the Crust:** Bake crust at 375°F (190°C) for 10 minutes.
2. **Make the Filling:** Whisk eggs, cream, cheese, bacon, salt, pepper, and nutmeg.
3. **Bake:** Pour into crust and bake for 30-35 minutes until set. Serve warm.

Croque Monsieur (French Ham & Cheese Sandwich)

Ingredients:

- 4 slices of bread
- 2 tbsp butter
- 2 tbsp all-purpose flour
- 1 cup milk
- ½ cup Gruyère cheese, shredded
- 4 slices ham
- Dijon mustard

Instructions:

1. **Make the Béchamel:** Melt butter, stir in flour, then slowly add milk to create a sauce. Stir in half the cheese.
2. **Assemble the Sandwich:** Spread mustard on bread, add ham and cheese, and top with another slice.
3. **Bake & Broil:** Bake at 375°F (190°C) for 10 minutes, then broil until golden brown.

Croque Madame (Croque Monsieur with an Egg)

Croque Madame (Classic French Ham & Cheese Sandwich with a Fried Egg)

Ingredients:

- 4 slices of bread (preferably brioche or country bread)
- 2 tbsp butter
- 2 tbsp all-purpose flour
- 1 cup milk
- ½ cup Gruyère cheese, shredded
- 4 slices ham
- 2 tsp Dijon mustard
- 2 fried eggs
- Salt and freshly ground black pepper (to taste)

Instructions:

1. **Make the Béchamel Sauce:**
    - In a small saucepan, melt 1 tbsp butter over medium heat.
    - Stir in flour and cook for 1 minute.
    - Slowly whisk in milk and cook until thickened.
    - Stir in half of the shredded Gruyère cheese, season with salt and pepper, then set aside.
2. **Assemble the Sandwiches:**
    - Spread Dijon mustard on two slices of bread.
    - Place ham on top, then add some béchamel sauce and a sprinkle of Gruyère cheese.
    - Top with another slice of bread.
3. **Toast the Sandwiches:**
    - Melt 1 tbsp butter in a pan over medium heat.
    - Cook sandwiches for 2-3 minutes per side until golden brown.
4. **Broil with Cheese:**
    - Transfer sandwiches to a baking sheet, top with more béchamel sauce and the remaining Gruyère cheese.
    - Broil for 2-3 minutes until bubbly and golden.
5. **Fry the Eggs:**
    - In a separate pan, fry two eggs sunny-side up.
6. **Serve:**
    - Place a fried egg on top of each sandwich and serve warm.

Tartiflette (Savory Potato & Cheese Casserole)

Ingredients:

- 2 lbs potatoes, sliced
- 1 small onion, chopped
- 6 oz bacon, cooked and crumbled
- 1 cup heavy cream
- 1 Reblochon cheese, sliced
- Salt and pepper to taste

Instructions:

1. **Sauté Onions & Bacon:** Cook together until soft.
2. **Layer & Bake:** In a baking dish, layer potatoes, bacon mixture, cream, and top with Reblochon cheese.
3. **Bake:** Cook at 375°F (190°C) for 30 minutes until golden and bubbly.

Salade Niçoise (Classic French Salad)

Ingredients:

- 2 cups mixed greens
- 1 cup green beans, blanched
- 2 hard-boiled eggs, sliced
- ½ cup cherry tomatoes, halved
- ½ cup black olives
- 1 can tuna, drained
- 4 small boiled potatoes, halved
- 2 tbsp olive oil
- 1 tbsp red wine vinegar
- 1 tsp Dijon mustard

Instructions:

1. **Assemble Salad:** Arrange greens, beans, eggs, tomatoes, olives, tuna, and potatoes.
2. **Make Dressing:** Whisk olive oil, vinegar, and mustard.
3. **Dress & Serve:** Drizzle over salad and serve chilled.

Chateaubriand Steak (Classic French Beef Tenderloin)

Ingredients:

- 1 lb beef tenderloin
- Salt and freshly ground black pepper
- 2 tbsp butter
- 1 tbsp olive oil
- 2 cloves garlic, minced
- 2 sprigs fresh thyme
- ½ cup red wine

Instructions:

1. **Season & Sear:** Rub beef with salt and pepper, sear in butter and oil.
2. **Roast:** Transfer to 375°F (190°C) oven for 15 minutes.
3. **Make Sauce:** Deglaze pan with red wine, add garlic and thyme, reduce until thick.
4. **Serve:** Slice steak and drizzle with sauce.

French Onion Soup

Ingredients:

- 4 large onions, thinly sliced
- 3 tbsp butter
- 1 tbsp olive oil
- 4 cups beef broth
- ½ cup dry white wine
- 1 tbsp Worcestershire sauce
- 1 tsp thyme
- Baguette slices
- 1 cup Gruyère cheese, shredded

Instructions:

1. **Caramelize Onions:** Cook onions in butter and oil over low heat for 40 minutes.
2. **Simmer:** Add broth, wine, Worcestershire sauce, and thyme. Simmer for 20 minutes.
3. **Toast Bread:** Place baguette slices in oven until golden.
4. **Assemble & Broil:** Pour soup into bowls, top with bread and cheese, then broil until bubbly.

Blanquette de Veau (French Veal Stew in White Sauce)

Ingredients:

- 2 lbs veal shoulder, cubed
- 4 cups veal or chicken broth
- 1 onion, studded with 2 cloves
- 2 carrots, sliced
- 2 celery stalks, chopped
- 1 bay leaf
- 4 sprigs thyme
- 8 oz button mushrooms, sliced
- ½ cup heavy cream
- 2 tbsp butter
- 2 tbsp flour
- 1 egg yolk
- Salt and pepper to taste
- Fresh parsley for garnish

Instructions:

1. **Simmer the Veal:** In a pot, cover veal with broth, add onion, carrots, celery, bay leaf, and thyme. Simmer for 1.5 hours.
2. **Prepare Mushrooms:** Sauté mushrooms in butter until tender.
3. **Make the Sauce:** Melt butter, stir in flour, then whisk in strained broth to make a velvety sauce.
4. **Combine & Serve:** Stir in heavy cream and egg yolk, return veal and mushrooms, and serve over rice.

Sole Meunière (Pan-Fried Sole with Butter & Lemon)

Ingredients:

- 2 sole fillets
- ½ cup flour
- Salt and pepper to taste
- 2 tbsp butter
- 2 tbsp olive oil
- 1 lemon, juiced
- 2 tbsp fresh parsley, chopped

Instructions:

1. **Coat the Fish:** Season fillets, dredge lightly in flour, and shake off excess.
2. **Sauté:** Heat oil and 1 tbsp butter, fry sole for 2-3 minutes per side.
3. **Make the Sauce:** Melt remaining butter, add lemon juice and parsley.
4. **Serve:** Drizzle sauce over fish and serve with steamed vegetables.

Pissaladière (French Onion and Anchovy Tart)

Ingredients:

- 1 sheet puff pastry
- 2 large onions, sliced
- 2 tbsp olive oil
- 1 tbsp butter
- 1 tsp thyme
- 10 anchovy fillets
- 12 black olives, halved

Instructions:

1. **Caramelize Onions:** Cook onions in butter and oil for 30 minutes until golden.
2. **Assemble Tart:** Spread onions over pastry, arrange anchovies and olives.
3. **Bake:** Cook at 375°F (190°C) for 20-25 minutes.

Pot-au-Feu (French Beef Stew)

Ingredients:

- 2 lbs beef brisket or short ribs
- 4 cups beef broth
- 2 carrots, peeled and cut
- 2 leeks, chopped
- 2 potatoes, peeled and halved
- 1 onion, studded with 2 cloves
- 2 cloves garlic
- 1 bouquet garni (thyme, bay leaf, parsley)
- Salt and pepper to taste

Instructions:

1. **Simmer the Meat:** Cover beef with broth, add garlic, onion, and bouquet garni. Cook for 2 hours.
2. **Add Vegetables:** Add carrots, leeks, and potatoes, simmer for 45 more minutes.
3. **Serve:** Slice beef and serve with broth and mustard.

Brandade de Morue (Salt Cod Purée)

Ingredients:

- 1 lb salt cod, soaked overnight
- 2 cups milk
- 2 garlic cloves, minced
- ½ cup olive oil
- 1 lemon, juiced
- 2 tbsp heavy cream
- Black pepper to taste

Instructions:

1. **Poach Cod:** Simmer cod in milk with garlic for 10 minutes.
2. **Mash & Blend:** Drain and mash cod, mix with olive oil, cream, and lemon juice until creamy.
3. **Serve:** Spread on bread or use as a dip.

Poulet Basquaise (Basque-Style Chicken)

Ingredients:

- 4 chicken thighs
- 1 onion, sliced
- 1 red bell pepper, sliced
- 1 green bell pepper, sliced
- 3 tomatoes, chopped
- 3 cloves garlic, minced
- ½ cup white wine
- 1 tsp smoked paprika
- 2 tbsp olive oil
- Salt and pepper to taste

Instructions:

1. **Brown the Chicken:** Sear chicken in olive oil, then set aside.
2. **Cook Vegetables:** Sauté onions, peppers, tomatoes, and garlic.
3. **Simmer:** Add white wine and paprika, return chicken, and cook for 30 minutes.

Tarte Tatin (Caramelized Upside-Down Apple Tart)

Ingredients:

- 4 apples, peeled and sliced
- ½ cup sugar
- 4 tbsp butter
- 1 sheet puff pastry

Instructions:

1. **Caramelize Apples:** Cook apples in sugar and butter until golden.
2. **Assemble:** Place apples in a baking dish, top with puff pastry.
3. **Bake:** Cook at 375°F (190°C) for 30 minutes, then invert onto a plate.

Mille-Feuille (Napoleon Pastry)

Ingredients:

- 1 sheet puff pastry
- 2 cups pastry cream
- ½ cup powdered sugar
- ½ cup dark chocolate, melted

Instructions:

1. **Bake Puff Pastry:** Roll and bake at 375°F (190°C) until golden.
2. **Layer with Pastry Cream:** Alternate layers of pastry and cream.
3. **Decorate:** Drizzle with melted chocolate and powdered sugar.

Crêpes Suzette (French Orange-Flambéed Crêpes)

Ingredients:

- 1 cup flour
- 2 eggs
- 1 cup milk
- 2 tbsp melted butter
- 2 tbsp sugar
- ½ cup orange juice
- ¼ cup Grand Marnier
- 2 tbsp sugar (for sauce)
- 2 tbsp butter

Instructions:

1. **Make Crêpes:** Mix batter, cook thin pancakes in a pan.
2. **Prepare Sauce:** Heat butter, sugar, and orange juice.
3. **Flambé:** Add Grand Marnier, ignite carefully, and drizzle over crêpes.

Madeleines (French Shell-Shaped Butter Cakes)

Ingredients:

- ½ cup butter, melted
- 2 eggs
- ½ cup sugar
- ¾ cup flour
- 1 tsp baking powder
- 1 tsp vanilla extract

Instructions:

1. **Mix Batter:** Whisk eggs and sugar, fold in flour, baking powder, and butter.
2. **Chill & Bake:** Refrigerate for 1 hour, then bake in a madeleine mold at 375°F (190°C) for 10 minutes.

Clafoutis (French Cherry Baked Custard)

Ingredients:

- 1 cup cherries (pitted)
- ½ cup all-purpose flour
- ½ cup sugar
- 3 eggs
- 1 cup milk
- 1 tsp vanilla extract
- 1 pinch salt
- 1 tbsp butter (for greasing)

Instructions:

1. **Preheat Oven:** Set to 375°F (190°C). Butter a baking dish.
2. **Make Batter:** Whisk flour, sugar, eggs, milk, vanilla, and salt until smooth.
3. **Assemble & Bake:** Pour batter over cherries in the dish and bake for 35 minutes.
4. **Serve:** Dust with powdered sugar and serve warm.

Pâté en Croûte (Pâté in Pastry Crust)

Ingredients:

- 1 sheet puff pastry
- 1 lb ground pork
- ½ lb ground veal
- 1 egg
- 2 tbsp brandy
- 2 cloves garlic, minced
- 1 tsp salt
- ½ tsp black pepper
- 1 tbsp fresh thyme

Instructions:

1. **Mix Filling:** Combine pork, veal, egg, brandy, garlic, salt, pepper, and thyme.
2. **Assemble:** Line a loaf pan with pastry, fill with meat mixture, and cover with another pastry sheet.
3. **Bake:** Cook at 375°F (190°C) for 45 minutes.

Escargots de Bourgogne (Burgundy Snails in Garlic Butter)

Ingredients:

- 12 escargots (cooked and cleaned)
- 4 tbsp butter, softened
- 2 cloves garlic, minced
- 1 tbsp parsley, chopped
- 1 tsp lemon juice
- Salt and pepper to taste

Instructions:

1. **Make Garlic Butter:** Mix butter, garlic, parsley, lemon juice, salt, and pepper.
2. **Fill Shells:** Place snails back in shells or ramekins and top with garlic butter.
3. **Bake:** Cook at 375°F (190°C) for 10 minutes until bubbly. Serve hot.

Hachis Parmentier (French Shepherd's Pie)

Ingredients:

- 1 lb ground beef
- 1 onion, chopped
- 2 cloves garlic, minced
- 2 cups mashed potatoes
- ½ cup milk
- 2 tbsp butter
- ½ cup grated Gruyère cheese
- Salt and pepper to taste

Instructions:

1. **Cook Meat:** Sauté beef, onion, and garlic until browned.
2. **Prepare Mashed Potatoes:** Mix mashed potatoes with milk and butter.
3. **Assemble & Bake:** Layer meat, then mashed potatoes in a baking dish. Top with cheese and bake at 375°F (190°C) for 20 minutes.

Andouillette (French Pork Sausage)

Ingredients:

- 2 Andouillette sausages
- 1 tbsp butter
- 1 tbsp Dijon mustard
- ½ cup white wine
- ½ cup heavy cream

Instructions:

1. **Sear Sausages:** Brown sausages in butter over medium heat.
2. **Make Sauce:** Deglaze with white wine, stir in mustard and cream.
3. **Simmer & Serve:** Cook for 5 minutes, then serve with potatoes.

Soufflé au Fromage (Cheese Soufflé)

Ingredients:

- 3 tbsp butter
- 3 tbsp flour
- 1 cup milk
- ½ cup Gruyère cheese, grated
- 3 eggs, separated
- Salt and pepper to taste

Instructions:

1. **Make Béchamel:** Melt butter, stir in flour, then whisk in milk.
2. **Add Cheese & Yolks:** Stir in cheese and egg yolks.
3. **Whip Egg Whites:** Beat whites to stiff peaks and fold into mixture.
4. **Bake:** Pour into a greased soufflé dish and bake at 375°F (190°C) for 25 minutes.

Choucroute Garnie (Alsatian Sauerkraut & Sausages)

Ingredients:

- 4 sausages (Bratwurst or Frankfurter)
- 1 lb sauerkraut
- 4 slices bacon
- 1 onion, sliced
- 2 cloves garlic, minced
- ½ cup white wine
- 1 bay leaf
- 1 tbsp juniper berries

Instructions:

1. **Cook Onions & Bacon:** Sauté in a large pot.
2. **Simmer:** Add sauerkraut, wine, bay leaf, juniper berries, and simmer for 30 minutes.
3. **Add Sausages:** Cook for 10 minutes and serve with potatoes.

Tarte Flambée (Alsatian Bacon & Onion Flatbread)

Ingredients:

- 1 pizza dough
- ½ cup crème fraîche
- 1 onion, thinly sliced
- 4 slices bacon, chopped
- Salt and pepper to taste

Instructions:

1. **Preheat Oven:** Set to 450°F (230°C).
2. **Assemble:** Roll out dough, spread crème fraîche, top with onions and bacon.
3. **Bake:** Cook for 15 minutes until crispy.

Boudin Noir aux Pommes (Blood Sausage with Apples)

Ingredients:

- 2 blood sausages (boudin noir)
- 2 apples, sliced
- 2 tbsp butter
- 1 tbsp honey
- Salt and pepper to taste

Instructions:

1. **Sauté Apples:** Cook in butter and honey until caramelized.
2. **Cook Sausage:** Sear blood sausages in a pan until heated through.
3. **Serve:** Plate sausage with apples and serve warm.

Rillettes de Porc (French Pork Spread)

Ingredients:

- 1 lb pork shoulder, cubed
- 1 cup pork fat
- 2 cloves garlic, minced
- 1 tsp salt
- ½ tsp black pepper
- 1 bay leaf
- ½ cup white wine

Instructions:

1. **Slow Cook Pork:** Simmer pork with fat, garlic, wine, and bay leaf for 3 hours.
2. **Shred & Mix:** Remove bay leaf, shred pork, and mix with its own fat.
3. **Chill & Serve:** Refrigerate until set, then spread on bread.

Oeufs en Meurette (Poached Eggs in Red Wine Sauce)

Ingredients:

- 4 eggs
- 2 cups red wine (Burgundy or Pinot Noir)
- ½ cup beef broth
- 4 slices bacon, chopped
- 1 small onion, chopped
- 2 cloves garlic, minced
- 1 tbsp butter
- 1 tbsp flour
- Salt and pepper to taste
- 4 slices toasted bread

Instructions:

1. **Prepare the Sauce:** Sauté bacon, onion, and garlic in butter. Sprinkle with flour, then add wine and broth. Simmer until thickened.
2. **Poach the Eggs:** In simmering water, poach eggs for 3 minutes until whites are set.
3. **Serve:** Place eggs on toast, spoon sauce over, and serve warm.

Pâté de Campagne (Rustic Country Pâté)

Ingredients:

- 1 lb ground pork
- ½ lb chicken liver, finely chopped
- 2 cloves garlic, minced
- 1 small onion, chopped
- 2 tbsp Cognac or brandy
- 1 tsp thyme
- 1 tsp salt
- ½ tsp black pepper
- 1 egg
- ½ cup heavy cream

Instructions:

1. **Mix Ingredients:** Combine all ingredients in a bowl until well blended.
2. **Bake:** Transfer to a loaf pan and bake at 350°F (175°C) for 1.5 hours.
3. **Chill & Serve:** Refrigerate overnight before slicing. Serve with baguette and pickles.

Frisée aux Lardons (Frisée Salad with Bacon and Poached Egg)

Ingredients:

- 4 cups frisée lettuce
- 4 slices bacon, chopped
- 2 tbsp red wine vinegar
- 1 tbsp Dijon mustard
- 4 eggs (poached)
- Salt and pepper to taste

Instructions:

1. **Cook Bacon:** Sauté bacon until crispy.
2. **Make Dressing:** Deglaze pan with vinegar, whisk in mustard, then toss with lettuce.
3. **Serve:** Top salad with poached eggs and crispy bacon.

Gâteau Basque (Basque Cake with Almond Custard Filling)

Ingredients:

- 2 cups flour
- ½ cup sugar
- 1 tsp baking powder
- ½ cup butter, softened
- 2 eggs
- 1 tsp vanilla extract
- 1 cup pastry cream
- ¼ cup cherry jam (optional)

Instructions:

1. **Make Dough:** Mix flour, sugar, baking powder, butter, eggs, and vanilla. Chill for 1 hour.
2. **Assemble:** Roll out half the dough, spread pastry cream and jam, then cover with remaining dough.
3. **Bake:** Cook at 350°F (175°C) for 35 minutes.

Île Flottante (Floating Island Dessert)

Ingredients:

- 4 egg whites
- ½ cup sugar
- 2 cups milk
- 1 tsp vanilla extract
- ½ cup caramel sauce

Instructions:

1. **Make Meringue:** Beat egg whites with sugar until stiff peaks form.
2. **Poach Meringues:** Simmer spoonfuls of meringue in hot milk for 2 minutes per side.
3. **Assemble & Serve:** Place poached meringues on vanilla-flavored milk and drizzle with caramel.

Pain Perdu (French Toast)

Ingredients:

- 4 slices brioche
- 2 eggs
- ½ cup milk
- 1 tbsp sugar
- ½ tsp cinnamon
- 1 tbsp butter
- Maple syrup for serving

Instructions:

1. **Make Batter:** Whisk eggs, milk, sugar, and cinnamon.
2. **Soak Bread:** Dip brioche slices into the mixture.
3. **Cook:** Fry in butter until golden brown. Serve with syrup.

Crème Brûlée (Classic Caramelized Custard)

Ingredients:

- 2 cups heavy cream
- 4 egg yolks
- ½ cup sugar
- 1 tsp vanilla extract
- 2 tbsp sugar (for caramel topping)

Instructions:

1. **Make Custard:** Heat cream, whisk in egg yolks, sugar, and vanilla.
2. **Bake:** Pour into ramekins and bake in a water bath at 325°F (160°C) for 45 minutes.
3. **Caramelize:** Sprinkle sugar on top and torch until golden.

Galettes Bretonnes (Buckwheat Crêpes from Brittany)

Ingredients:

- 1 cup buckwheat flour
- 1 egg
- 1 cup water
- 1 tbsp melted butter
- ½ tsp salt

Instructions:

1. **Make Batter:** Whisk all ingredients together and let rest for 30 minutes.
2. **Cook Crêpes:** Pour batter into a hot greased pan and cook for 2 minutes per side.
3. **Fill & Serve:** Add cheese, ham, or eggs as desired.

Boulette d'Avesnes (Spiced French Cheese Ball)

Ingredients:

- 1 cup fresh cow's milk cheese (or mix of Maroilles and butter)
- 1 tbsp paprika
- 1 tbsp cayenne pepper
- 1 tsp salt
- 1 tsp black pepper

Instructions:

1. **Mix Ingredients:** Combine cheese with spices until smooth.
2. **Shape & Age:** Form into a ball and let age for a few days.
3. **Serve:** Slice and enjoy with rustic bread.

Gratin Dauphinois (Creamy French Potato Gratin)

Ingredients:

- 2 lbs potatoes, thinly sliced
- 1 cup heavy cream
- 1 cup milk
- 2 cloves garlic, minced
- ½ cup Gruyère cheese, grated
- Salt and pepper to taste

Instructions:

1. **Preheat Oven:** Set to 375°F (190°C).
2. **Layer Potatoes:** Arrange in a baking dish with garlic, cream, and cheese.
3. **Bake:** Cook for 45 minutes until golden brown.

Saucisson Lyonnais (Lyon-Style Sausage with Potatoes)

Ingredients:

- 1 Lyon-style saucisson (or smoked sausage)
- 4 medium potatoes, peeled and sliced
- 1 onion, thinly sliced
- 2 tbsp butter
- ½ cup white wine
- 1 bay leaf
- Salt and pepper to taste

Instructions:

1. **Cook the Sausage:** Poach the saucisson in simmering water for 30 minutes.
2. **Prepare Potatoes:** Sauté onions in butter, add potatoes, wine, bay leaf, salt, and pepper. Cover and cook for 20 minutes.
3. **Slice & Serve:** Slice the sausage and serve over the potatoes.

Daube Provençale (Provençal Beef Stew with Red Wine)

Ingredients:

- 2 lbs beef chuck, cubed
- 1 onion, sliced
- 2 carrots, sliced
- 3 cloves garlic, minced
- 2 cups red wine (Côtes du Rhône or Syrah)
- 1 cup beef broth
- 1 tbsp tomato paste
- 2 sprigs thyme
- 1 bay leaf
- 2 tbsp olive oil
- Salt and pepper to taste

Instructions:

1. **Marinate Beef:** Combine beef, wine, garlic, thyme, and bay leaf. Marinate overnight.
2. **Brown Meat:** Sauté meat in olive oil, add onions, carrots, and tomato paste.
3. **Slow Cook:** Add marinade and broth, cover, and simmer for 3 hours. Serve with crusty bread.

Navarin d'Agneau (French Spring Lamb Stew)

Ingredients:

- 2 lbs lamb shoulder, cubed
- 2 carrots, peeled and sliced
- 2 potatoes, diced
- 1 onion, chopped
- 2 cloves garlic, minced
- 2 cups beef or chicken broth
- ½ cup white wine
- 1 tbsp tomato paste
- 2 sprigs thyme
- 1 bay leaf
- 2 tbsp olive oil
- Salt and pepper to taste

Instructions:

1. **Brown the Lamb:** Sear lamb in olive oil, then set aside.
2. **Sauté Aromatics:** Cook onions, garlic, and carrots.
3. **Simmer:** Add lamb, broth, wine, tomato paste, thyme, and bay leaf. Cook for 1.5 hours.
4. **Add Potatoes:** Stir in potatoes and simmer for 30 minutes more. Serve warm.

Gigot d'Agneau (Roast Leg of Lamb with Garlic & Herbs)

Ingredients:

- 1 bone-in leg of lamb (about 5 lbs)
- 4 cloves garlic, sliced
- 2 tbsp olive oil
- 2 tbsp Dijon mustard
- 1 tbsp rosemary, chopped
- 1 tbsp thyme, chopped
- Salt and pepper to taste

Instructions:

1. **Prepare the Lamb:** Make small incisions in the meat and insert garlic slices.
2. **Season:** Rub with olive oil, mustard, rosemary, thyme, salt, and pepper.
3. **Roast:** Cook at 375°F (190°C) for about 1.5 hours (medium-rare). Let rest for 15 minutes before slicing.

Vol-au-Vent (Puff Pastry Shells with Creamy Filling)

Ingredients:

- 1 sheet puff pastry
- 2 tbsp butter
- 2 tbsp flour
- 1 cup milk
- ½ cup mushrooms, chopped
- ½ cup cooked chicken, shredded
- Salt and pepper to taste

Instructions:

1. **Bake Pastry:** Cut circles from puff pastry and bake at 375°F (190°C) until golden.
2. **Make Filling:** Sauté mushrooms, add butter, flour, and milk to make a thick sauce. Stir in chicken.
3. **Assemble & Serve:** Fill pastry shells with creamy mixture and serve warm.

Aligot (French Mashed Potatoes with Cheese)

Ingredients:

- 2 lbs potatoes, peeled and diced
- 1 cup heavy cream
- 2 tbsp butter
- 2 cups Tomme cheese (or Gruyère), shredded
- 2 cloves garlic, minced
- Salt and pepper to taste

Instructions:

1. **Boil Potatoes:** Cook in salted water until soft, then mash.
2. **Add Dairy:** Stir in butter, cream, and garlic.
3. **Incorporate Cheese:** Gradually mix in cheese, stirring until smooth and stretchy.

Canard à l'Orange (French Duck with Orange Sauce)

Ingredients:

- 2 duck breasts
- ½ cup orange juice
- 1 orange, zested
- 2 tbsp honey
- 2 tbsp balsamic vinegar
- ½ cup chicken broth
- Salt and pepper to taste

Instructions:

1. **Sear the Duck:** Score duck skin, season with salt, and cook skin-side down until crispy. Flip and cook for 5 minutes.
2. **Make the Sauce:** In a pan, reduce orange juice, zest, honey, vinegar, and broth.
3. **Serve:** Slice duck and drizzle with sauce.